Owen Farrel

C000148401

Chapters:

Owen Farrell

Introduction

Welcome to the thrilling world of "Rugby Heroes: Owen Farrell," the inaugural instalment in a series that unveils the extraordinary tales of the world's greatest rugby players. In these pages, we invite you to step onto the hallowed turf and join us on a captivating journey through the life and career of one of rugby's most iconic figures.

Owen Farrell, a name synonymous with passion, resilience, and unyielding determination, has carved a path through the rugby world that transcends mere sporting achievement. This biography, tailored for young adults, peels back the layers of Farrell's story, revealing the defining moments, triumphs, and trials that have shaped him into the formidable athlete and leader he is today.

From the early days of childhood dreams to captaining the England national team, Farrell's journey is a testament to the indomitable spirit of rugby. As we traverse the chapters of this book, you'll witness the highs of unforgettable victories, the lows of heart-wrenching defeats, and the unwavering commitment that defines a true rugby hero.

Beyond the boundaries of the pitch, Owen Farrell's story offers more than a glimpse into the world of sports—it's a narrative of leadership, teamwork, and the pursuit of excellence. As we delve into his experiences, we discover the character of a young man who not only plays with heart but inspires those around him to do the same.

Whether you're a dedicated rugby enthusiast or simply seeking an inspiring story of triumph over adversity, "Rugby Heroes: Owen Farrell" promises an immersive and heartfelt experience. Join us as we celebrate the life and legacy of a true rugby legend, and embark on a journey that goes beyond the try line, into the heart of one of rugby's most celebrated heroes. Are you ready to be inspired, challenged, and moved by the story of Owen Farrell's rise to greatness? Let the journey begin.

Owen Farrell

Chapter 1: The Early Years

In the picturesque town of Wigan, a young Owen Farrell, born on September 24, 1991, embarked on his journey into the world of rugby—a legacy deeply embedded in his genes. The Farrell household, led by his father, Andy Farrell, a former rugby league and union player turned coach, provided the nurturing grounds for Owen's early exposure to the sport.

Owen's early years were steeped in the culture of rugby. The son of a renowned rugby figure, his fascination with the game was kindled at a young age. This chapter of his life unfolded against the backdrop of local rugby clubs, where

Owen Farrell

muddy boots and laughter filled weekends, laying the foundation for a lifelong connection to the sport.

As a child, Owen's passion for rugby blossomed. His early forays onto the pitch showcased a natural talent that set him apart. The local club became a second home, a place where dreams of a burgeoning rugby career began to take shape.

The Farrell household, as described in various sources, was a hub of rugby enthusiasm. With a father who had donned the jerseys of prominent rugby teams, young Owen was surrounded by an environment that fuelled his love for the game. His formative years were not just marked by backyard games but by the

invaluable lessons imbibed from the rich rugby heritage of the Farrell family.

This chapter encapsulates the early years of a young boy whose destiny intertwined with the oval ball. From childhood dreams to the promising horizon of a rugby career, Owen Farrell's journey had just commenced. Little did he know that the pages of his story would unfold on local pitches and eventually lead him to the grand stages of international rugby.

Chapter 2: A Rugby Journey Begins

In the quaint town of Wigan, a young Owen Farrell embarked on a rugby journey that would shape his destiny. Born into a rugby-centric family, his early years were steeped in the traditions of the sport. Farrell's boyhood teams, where his talents began to flourish, painted the canvas of a future rugby luminary.

As a youth, Farrell joined the famed Orrell RUFC, a club with a rich history and a reputation for nurturing emerging rugby talents. Here, on the hallowed grounds of Edge Hall Road, the foundations of his rugby prowess were laid. The camaraderie forged in the junior ranks of Orrell

would become an integral part of his formative years.

The allure of the oval ball and the thrill of competition soon led Farrell to further hone his skills at the Wigan St Patricks Amateur Rugby League Football Club. This transition marked a pivotal juncture in his early rugby education. The St Patricks Club, deeply embedded in the local rugby scene, provided an environment where Farrell could refine his technique and develop the resilience that would later define his playing style.

As the pages of his youth turned, so did the trajectory of Farrell's rugby journey. The boy who once donned the jerseys of Orrell RUFC and Wigan St Patricks was gradually evolving into a player of immense promise. Little did the young Farrell realize that these humble beginnings would serve as the launching pad for a career that would take him to the pinnacles of rugby success.

Chapter 2 unfolds with the echoes of cheers from local spectators, the camaraderie of teammates, and the undeniable passion that marked Owen Farrell's earliest encounters with the sport. These boyhood teams, deeply woven into the fabric of his youth, set the stage for the remarkable odyssey that awaited the young rugby enthusiast from Wigan.

Chapter 3: Passion Ignited

As Owen Farrell's journey progressed, a fiery passion for rugby ignited within him, casting a brilliant glow on the path ahead. The transition from local matches to more competitive arenas didn't diminish his enthusiasm; instead, it fuelled a burning desire to excel and leave an indelible mark on the sport he loved.

The intensity of Owen's commitment to rugby was matched only by his insatiable hunger for improvement. He spent countless hours honing his skills, refining his technique, and absorbing the wisdom of coaches who recognized the burgeoning talent in their midst. The training

grounds became a second home, and the echoes of his boots pounding against the grass signalled not just effort, but a relentless pursuit of perfection.

As Owen ascended through the ranks, the challenges became steeper, the opposition more formidable. Yet, with each hurdle, he discovered reserves of resilience and determination that set him apart. The taste of victory, sweet and hard-earned, fuelled his appetite for success, while defeats became valuable lessons, etching into his character the importance of perseverance in the face of adversity.

The rugby community at large began to take notice of the young player whose passion for

the game radiated from every tackle, every scrum, and every sprint down the field. His performances spoke volumes, and the thrill of competition became the crucible in which his character was forged. Beyond the physicality of the sport, Owen's leadership qualities emerged, commanding the respect of teammates and opponents alike.

Off the pitch, his commitment extended beyond personal glory. Owen became involved in community initiatives, sharing his love for rugby with the next generation of players. The rugby field transformed into a classroom where he imparted not only technical skills but the values of sportsmanship, teamwork, and dedication that had shaped his own journey.

Owen Farrell

As the flames of passion roared within him, Owen Farrell stood at the precipice of a promising future.

Chapter 4: The Rise to Prominence

In the small town of Wigan, Owen Farrell's journey through the rugby ranks began to take an extraordinary turn. As his skills on the field continued to blossom, whispers of his remarkable talent began to circulate beyond the local rugby clubs. A palpable buzz surrounded the young player, and with each match, his prowess became increasingly evident.

Farrell's standout performances in the youth leagues drew attention, not just from the local rugby enthusiasts but from scouts and pundits who recognized the exceptional potential within him. The precision of his kicks, the strategic acumen displayed on the pitch, and his innate leadership qualities caught the eye of those well-versed in identifying rugby's rising stars.

As accolades piled up and victories under his leadership mounted, the clamour for Owen Farrell to step into the professional league became a resonant chorus. Calls from rugby pundits, coaches, and even seasoned players echoed the sentiment that Farrell's skill set was too prodigious to be confined to the amateur ranks. The town that had witnessed his early endeavours now eagerly awaited the next chapter in the remarkable story of the local rugby prodigy.

The prospect of Farrell joining the professional league wasn't merely a speculative notion; it was a testament to his undeniable impact on the sport. The local hero had transcended the boundaries of youth and amateur rugby, and a broader stage beckoned—one where his talents could be showcased on a grander scale.

This chapter unfolds with the excitement and anticipation that surrounded Owen Farrell's ascent. The air was charged with the promise of a future where the boy from Wigan, with his remarkable skills and leadership, would make a mark in the professional league, leaving an indelible imprint on the world of rugby. The calls for his ascent were not just echoes in the wind; they were the heralds of a journey poised for new heights and greater challenges.

Chapter 5: The Professional Arena

The transition from national acclaim to the professional arena marked a pivotal juncture in Owen Farrell's journey. As he stepped onto the hallowed grounds of professional rugby, the stakes were higher, the competition fiercer, and the demands more exacting. The local hero had evolved into a seasoned player, ready to test his mettle against the best in the world.

Club rugby, with its gruelling schedules and international contingents, provided Owen with a new canvas on which to paint his rugby masterpiece. Joining the ranks of a prestigious club, he found himself surrounded by a cohort of top-tier athletes, each vying for success on domestic and international fronts. The camaraderie within the club became a melting pot of talents, a crucible in which individual brilliance merged with collective ambition.

The professional arena demanded more than just physical prowess; it required a mental fortitude to navigate the pressures of high-stakes matches, the expectations of fans, and the rigorous demands of a relentless season. Owen's approach, however, remained resolute. The hours spent on the training ground, analysing opponents, and fine-tuning his skills spoke to a player dedicated to continual improvement.

Owen Farrell

As he faced off against formidable opponents week after week, Owen's versatility became a prized asset. His ability to seamlessly switch between playmaking and goal-kicking roles showcased a player who could adapt to the dynamic ebb and flow of professional rugby. Each match unfolded like a chess game, with Owen orchestrating moves, making split-second decisions, and leaving an indelible mark on the scoreboard.

Victories in domestic competitions and standout performances on the European stage further solidified Owen's reputation as a force to be reckoned with. The local hero had seamlessly transitioned into a professional powerhouse, leaving an imprint not only on the stat sheets but on the hearts of fans who marvelled at his tenacity and skill.

Off the field, the demands of professionalism extended beyond the game itself. Media commitments, sponsor engagements, and the ever-watchful eyes of a global audience added layers of complexity to Owen's daily life. Yet, amidst the whirlwind, he remained grounded, acknowledging the responsibility that came with being a standard-bearer for both club and country.

As the professional chapters of Owen Farrell's career unfolded, the pages were filled with tales of resilience, triumph, and the relentless pursuit of excellence. The local hero had ventured into the professional arena, and with each match, he etched his name deeper into the annals of rugby history. Little did he know that the next chapters would bring new challenges, iconic moments, and a legacy that would resonate far beyond the try lines of the professional rugby stage.

Chapter 6: The Club Maestro

Before the iconic call-up to the England national team, Owen Farrell's ascent through the rugby ranks saw him carve out a sterling reputation at the club level. The journey that culminated in international recognition was paved with standout performances, leadership, and a relentless pursuit of excellence.

Farrell's foray into professional club rugby began with Saracens, a powerhouse in the English Premiership. Joining the senior squad at a young age, he quickly asserted himself as a key playmaker. His accurate kicking, tactical brilliance, and unwavering commitment on the field caught the attention of both teammates and rivals alike.

The Saracens jersey became a canvas for Farrell's rugby artistry. His ability to control the game, make crucial plays, and deliver under pressure marked him as a standout player in the English club scene. As he progressed through the ranks, he became a linchpin in Saracens' quest for Premiership glory.

Farrell's club career continued to flourish, and he showcased his versatility by seamlessly transitioning between fly-half and centre roles. His performances in domestic competitions and European tournaments solidified his status as one of the premier talents in English rugby.

A brief loan spell with Bedford Blues further honed his skills, providing valuable playing time and experiences that contributed to his overall development. The hunger for success that defined his youth now found a more expansive playground in the professional club arena.

The chapter unfolds with the resonance of Farrell's contributions at the club level, a testament to his mettle and determination. Each match became a stepping stone, and as the rugby world took notice of his prowess, the inevitability of an international call-up loomed on the horizon. The Saracens faithful, who had witnessed his rise, could sense that their maestro was on the cusp of a new and illustrious chapter in the storied journey of Owen Farrell.

Chapter 7: The England Call-Up

The turning point in Owen Farrell's burgeoning rugby career arrived with a seismic announcement—the call-up to the England national team. The date was February 11, 2012, etched in the annals of his journey as a moment that transcended club achievements and marked the inception of an international chapter.

As England prepared to face Scotland in the Six Nations Championship, the rugby world buzzed with anticipation. Farrell's inclusion in the matchday squad was not just a call-up; it was a validation of his exceptional talent and the realization of a childhood dream. The 20-year-old fly-half was set to make his debut on the grand stage of international rugby.

February 11, 2012, witnessed the culmination of years of dedication, hard work, and a relentless pursuit of excellence. The iconic white jersey adorned with the red rose was now Farrell's to wear—a symbol of national pride and a representation of the immense responsibilities bestowed upon an England player.

As the Twickenham Stadium roared with anticipation, Farrell made his debut against Scotland, stepping onto the pitch with a blend of nerves and excitement. The match unfolded as a showcase of his skill, composure, and a glimpse into the leadership qualities that would define his tenure with the national team.

The final whistle resonated with a victorious tone for England, and Farrell's debut was not just a personal triumph; it was a promising prelude to a remarkable international career. The boy who had honed his skills on the fields of Wigan and impressed at the club level had now officially announced his arrival on the international rugby scene.

Chapter 7 unfolds with the historic call-up and debut, a narrative punctuated by the roar of the Twickenham crowd and the symbolic weight of the England jersey on Owen Farrell's shoulders. Little did he know that this moment was the inception of a journey that would see him become a stalwart for England, leaving an indelible mark on the landscape of international rugby.

Chapter 8: Leadership Unveiled

The captain's armband, an emblem of leadership and responsibility, found its way onto Owen Farrell's arm, marking a new chapter in his journey. The evolution from local hero to national icon had reached a zenith as he assumed the role of captain for the England national rugby team. It wasn't just about wearing the armband; it was about shouldering the hopes and aspirations of a nation.

Stepping into the captaincy role, Owen embraced the challenge with a maturity that belied his years. The weight of leadership did not rest heavily; instead, it became a source of inspiration for both himself and his teammates. The huddle before a match, the motivating speeches in the locker room, and the strategic discussions on the training ground were now led by a captain whose commitment to excellence was unwavering.

On the field, Owen's leadership manifested in his style of play. A captain who led by example, he dove into tackles, orchestrated plays with finesse, and lifted the team during moments of adversity. The armband wasn't just an accessory; it was a symbol of the trust placed in him to guide England through the ebb and flow of international rugby.

Owen Farrell

Off the field, the responsibilities extended beyond the matchday arena. Owen became the face of the team, representing England in press conferences, engaging with fans, and fostering a sense of unity within the squad. The captaincy wasn't just about the 80 minutes on the field; it was a 24/7 commitment to the team's success and the legacy of the rose.

The challenges of captaincy were multifaceted – managing egos, navigating tactical decisions, and inspiring a diverse group of individuals with a common purpose. Owen's ability to strike a balance between camaraderie and authority earned him the respect of teammates and opposition alike. The captaincy, once a symbolic honour, now embodied the essence of Owen Farrell's leadership journey.

Owen Farrell

Triumphant victories and hard-fought battles under Owen's captaincy added a new layer to his legacy. The England national team, under his guidance, became a formidable force on the international stage. The chapters of his story were now adorned with the indelible mark of leadership – a mark that went beyond the try lines and resonated with fans who saw in him not just a captain but a symbol of inspiration.

As Owen Farrell continued to lead England with passion and purpose, the captain's armband became a crown of leadership, and the narrative of his journey unfolded with a promise of more victories, challenges, and the enduring legacy of a captain whose leadership defined an era of English rugby.

Chapter 9:
Triumphs and Trials

Chapter 9 of Owen Farrell's rugby journey is a narrative woven with the tapestry of triumphs and challenges that have defined his career. Notable victories, etched in the rugby archives, showcase Farrell's exceptional contributions to the sport. One such moment is the England vs. New Zealand clash in 2012, where Farrell's precision kicks and strategic brilliance played a pivotal role in England's historic 38-21 victory at Twickenham. This triumph underscored his mettle as both a player and a leader.

However, the narrative is not confined to victories alone. Trials and setbacks have shaped

Owen Farrell

Owen Farrell's story. In the 2015 Rugby World Cup, England faced a hard-fought defeat against Wales. The disappointment etched on Farrell's face after this closely contested match serves as a stark reminder that defeats are an inherent part of the rugby journey.

Evidence of physical trials is found in significant injuries Owen has faced. A notable instance is the ligament injury he sustained during the 2017 Six Nations Championship, leading to his absence from the remaining tournament matches. This injury became a turning point in his narrative, a moment of vulnerability that highlighted the physical toll and risks inherent in professional rugby. Owen's subsequent recovery and return to the pitch showcased not only his resilience but also his unwavering commitment to the sport.

As the pages turn, the narrative of triumphs and trials paints a nuanced picture of Owen Farrell's career. It is a journey marked by exceptional highs and humbling lows, a testament to his character and commitment to the game. These moments, documented in the records of his career, add depth to the legacy of a player who navigates both victories and setbacks with unwavering determination. As Chapter 9 unfolds, the anticipation grows for the next chapters, promising new challenges, iconic moments, and the continuation of a legacy forged in the crucible of triumphs and trials.

Owen Farrell slots over a conversion

Owen Farrell

Owen Farrell representing the British & Irish
Lions

Owen Farrell

A key member of the Saracens squad

Owen Farrell

Securing the Grand Slam 2016

Chapter 10: A Global Stage

The tenth chapter of Owen Farrell's illustrious rugby career unfurls against the backdrop of a global stage. No longer confined to the local fields or even the national arenas, Owen's journey had transcended borders, propelling him onto the grandest stages of international rugby.

One pinnacle of this global odyssey was the Rugby World Cup. The chapter opens with the 2015 tournament, a landmark moment in Owen's career. As England's playmaker and goal-kicker, the pressure on him was immense. The tournament witnessed Farrell's exceptional contributions and leadership. However, it also bore witness to the highs and lows inherent in the world's most prestigious rugby competition.

The subsequent World Cups, including the 2019 edition, marked Owen's evolution as a key figure on the international scene. His performances garnered attention not only for his individual skills but for his role in steering the England squad through the unpredictable waters of global competition. The intensity of World Cup matches, the camaraderie among players, and the weight of representing a nation on the global stage became defining elements of this chapter.

Beyond the World Cup, Owen's global impact extended to the British and Irish Lions tours.

Owen Farrell

The camaraderie forged with players from diverse backgrounds showcased not only his adaptability on the field but his ability to unite with fellow rugby warriors in pursuit of a common goal.

Triumphant victories in international test matches against rugby powerhouses and stellar performances in prestigious tournaments such as the Six Nations Championship added layers to Owen's global narrative. The statistics and match reports from these events stand testament to his enduring prowess as a playmaker and captain.

However, no global journey is devoid of challenges. The tenth chapter acknowledges the trials faced on this expansive stage.

Owen Farrell

Controversial moments, closely scrutinized decisions, and the unrelenting scrutiny of a global audience all become part of the tapestry. Yet, in the face of adversity, Owen's resilience shines through, showcasing a player who thrives on the grandest stages.

As Chapter 10 unfolds, the global stage becomes not just a setting but a crucible that molds Owen Farrell's legacy. The highs of triumphs and the lows of challenges paint a panoramic portrait of a player whose journey has left an indelible mark on the international rugby landscape. With each match, each tournament, and each global endeavor, the saga of Owen Farrell continues, promising more iconic moments and new chapters on the horizon.

Chapter 11: Off the Field

In the intimate chapters of Owen Farrell's life beyond the rugby pitch, the narrative extends to his personal realm, woven with threads of family, philanthropy, and a commitment to making a positive impact.

Family Values and Upbringing:

The exploration of Owen's upbringing extends beyond his parents to encompass his own family, with Georgie as a central figure. Their marriage in 2018 marks a significant milestone, and the couple has welcomed two sons into their lives. This family dynamic becomes a defining element in Owen's identity, shaping not only his rugby journey but also his approach to life. Interviews and profiles provide glimpses of a loving family man who finds strength and support in his roles as a husband and father.

Philanthropy and Charitable Initiatives:

Owen Farrell's commitment to philanthropy finds a deeper resonance when considering the support of the Matt Hampson Foundation. His active involvement in charitable causes extends beyond the rugby sphere and reflects a shared commitment with his wife, Georgie, to make a meaningful impact on the lives of others. Together, they contribute not only financially but also invest time and effort into initiatives that address various social issues. Their charitable work showcases a compassionate side of Owen, aligning with his desire to create positive change beyond the boundaries of the rugby field.

Chapter 12: Legacy in the Making

In the tapestry of Owen Farrell's career, Chapter 12 emerges as a nuanced exploration of the legacy he diligently crafts—a legacy that surpasses the try lines and jersey numbers, transcending the realms of rugby.

In the spotlight of leadership, Owen's captaincy becomes a focal point of this chapter. The armband isn't merely an accessory but a symbol of the profound impact he has had on Saracens and the England national team. Through strategic prowess, resilience in the face of adversity, and an unwavering ability to inspire, Owen's leadership legacy takes root in the annals of rugby history. Each match becomes a canvas where his captaincy paints a narrative of unity, determination, and a steadfast commitment to leading by example.

Yet, beyond the stadium lights and raucous cheers, Owen's legacy is intimately entwined with the quiet moments of family life. From his marriage to Georgie, a union that symbolizes partnership and support, to the laughter and lessons shared with their two sons, Owen's legacy extends into the foundations of family, grounding him in values that shape not only his character but also the narrative of his life beyond rugby.

Philanthropy stands as a pillar of Owen's legacy—a commitment that transcends the boundaries of the sport. Together with Georgie, their efforts reach far beyond financial contributions, encompassing hands-on engagement and a genuine desire to make a positive difference. It's a legacy built on compassion, empathy, and a recognition of the platform they hold to effect meaningful change.

As the narrative widens its scope, the global influence Owen exerts on the rugby landscape comes into focus. The legacy isn't confined to domestic victories but extends to the grand stages of international competition. World Cups, Six Nations triumphs, and the camaraderie forged in British and Irish Lions tours become chapters in a legacy written on the global canvas of rugby. Owen's impact resonates not just with teammates and opponents but with fans worldwide, etching his name into the collective memory of the sport.

Yet, the making of this legacy is not without its complexities. Balancing the demands of professional rugby, family life, and philanthropic endeavours requires a delicate equilibrium. It's a legacy not only of triumphs but of navigating setbacks with grace and determination, contributing to the holistic portrait of Owen Farrell.

As Chapter 12 unfolds, the legacy in the making becomes a mosaic, intricately woven with threads of leadership, family, philanthropy, and a global impact on the sport he loves. It is a story of a player whose influence extends far beyond the rugby pitch, promising a lasting legacy that resonates with fans, teammates, and the broader community—a legacy that continues to evolve with each chapter written on and off the field.

Chapter 13: Looking Ahead

In the twilight of his playing career, Owen Farrell stands at the crossroads of reflection and anticipation. Retirement looms, a contemplative journey into a future unscripted and uncertain. Questions of identity, purpose, and the transition from field dominance to uncharted realms shape the emotional landscape of this pivotal moment.

The prospect of Owen's continued influence in rugby takes prominence. Coaching emerges as a potential avenue, a conduit for him to share the wealth of knowledge accrued through years of elite competition. Whether as a mentor to emerging talents or a strategic mind shaping team dynamics, the unwritten rugby chapters of Owen Farrell beckon with a promise of ongoing impact.

Beyond the try lines, the philanthropic legacy crafted alongside Georgie takes on new dimensions. The narrative envisions the couple deepening their commitment to social causes, exploring avenues to leverage their influence for transformative change. Initiatives yet unexplored, partnerships awaiting formation— the philanthropic chapter unfolds with the potential to extend their positive influence far beyond rugby.

Family life, a recurring theme, continues its evolution. Owen navigates the intricacies of parenthood and marriage, and the Farrell family experiences new milestones. As their sons grow, the familial tapestry weaves together the legacy of love, resilience, and shared experiences that transcend the rugby field.

Looking ahead, the narrative acknowledges the unpredictable nature of the future. Owen's journey may involve unexpected ventures, uncharted territories, and challenges yet to be faced. The chapter invites readers into a speculative journey, pondering the myriad possibilities awaiting a man whose influence extends beyond the try lines. New passions may be discovered, fresh challenges embraced—the unwritten chapters hold the potential for continued growth, transformation, and a legacy that transcends the boundaries of sport.

Chapter 14: Records and Accolades

As Owen Farrell's illustrious rugby career unfolds, Chapter 14 turns its gaze to the numerous records and accolades that punctuate his journey. From his early days in local clubs to the international stage, Farrell's exceptional skill set and leadership have etched his name into the annals of rugby history.

International Accolades:

Farrell's international career with England is studded with achievements. He became the youngest England player to participate in a Rugby World Cup when he made his debut in the 2011 tournament. Over the years, he ascended to become one of England's most capped and decorated players, contributing significantly to the team's successes in the Six Nations Championship and other prestigious competitions.

Points Scoring Prowess:

A prolific scorer, Farrell's proficiency with the boot is evident in his point-scoring records. He holds records for most points scored by an English player in a single Six Nations Championship and is among the highest point-scorers in England's rugby history. His accurate kicking has been a cornerstone of many victories and a testament to his precision under pressure.

British and Irish Lions Success:

Farrell's impact extends beyond national borders, as he played a pivotal role in the British and Irish Lions tours. His performances in these esteemed tours contributed to series victories, adding another layer to his storied career and solidifying his reputation as a standout player on the global stage.

Individual Honors:

Individually, Farrell has been the recipient of numerous awards. Accolades such as the Six Nations Player of the Championship and nominations for prestigious awards like the

Owen Farrell

World Rugby Player of the Year underscore the recognition he has garnered for his outstanding contributions to the sport.

Captaincy and Leadership Milestones:

Taking the reins as the captain of the England national team marked a significant chapter in Farrell's career. Under his leadership, the team achieved notable successes, and he became one of the youngest players to captain England. His ability to lead with composure and inspire his teammates has left an indelible mark on England's rugby narrative.

As Chapter 14 unfurls, the narrative is adorned with the glittering achievements and milestones that define Owen Farrell's journey. Each record, award, and accolade speaks to a career marked by excellence, resilience, and an enduring commitment to the pursuit of rugby greatness. The accolades not only attest to Farrell's individual brilliance but also signify the collective triumphs of the teams he has led and the impact he has had on the sport at large.

Chapter 15: Bonus: The Game Beyond the Pitch

As Owen Farrell's narrative extends into Chapter 14, a departure from the personal tale takes centre stage. This chapter delves into the fascinating world of rugby, exploring its intricacies, quirks, and some delightful fun facts that underscore the sport's unique charm.

The Shape of the Ball:

Rugby, with its distinctive oval-shaped ball, stands out among the sea of spherical counterparts. But why the unique shape? The story goes that in the early days of the game, a pig's bladder was used as the ball. Its irregular shape led to the creation of the distinctive rugby ball we know today.

Origin of the Scrum:

The scrum, a defining element of rugby, has roots in a rather unexpected place—animal husbandry. The term "scrum" originates from the scrummage, a practice in which players bound together in a huddle, resembling the tight formation of a forward pack.

The Haka:

Rugby is not just about the game but the cultural richness it brings. The Haka, a traditional Maori war dance, is an integral part of New Zealand's rugby culture. The All Blacks, the national rugby team of New Zealand, perform the Haka before matches, adding a unique and powerful dimension to the sport.

Rugby's Global Reach:

While rugby's heartland is often associated with nations like New Zealand, South Africa, England, and Australia, the sport has a global footprint. Countries like Japan, Fiji, and Argentina have made significant strides in international competitions, showcasing rugby's ability to transcend geographical boundaries.

Rugby and the Moon:

In 1971, a small rubber rugby ball made its way to the moon with the Apollo 15 mission. Astronaut David Scott famously used it to demonstrate the difference in gravity between Earth and the moon, highlighting the peculiarities that make rugby a sport even astronauts can relate to.

Women in Rugby:

Rugby is not just a men's game. The Women's Rugby World Cup has been held since 1991, showcasing the incredible talent, skill, and dedication of female rugby players worldwide. The women's game continues to grow, challenging stereotypes and expanding the sport's reach.

Scoring with Style:

Rugby not only rewards physical prowess but also style and finesse. A drop goal, where a player kicks the ball through the posts in open play, is a testament to a player's skill and composure under pressure. Its rarity adds an element of surprise and excitement to the game.

As we explore these fun facts, Chapter 14 sheds light on the rich tapestry that is rugby—a sport that transcends borders, embraces tradition, and continues to evolve. The bonus chapter celebrates the intricacies that make rugby not just a game but a cultural phenomenon with a global impact.

Glossary

Captain's Armband: A symbolic accessory worn by the team captain, signifying leadership and responsibility on and off the rugby pitch.

Drop Goal: A method of scoring in rugby where a player kicks the ball through the goalposts during open play by dropping it to the ground and then kicking it as it rebounds.

Forward Pack: The group of players in a rugby team, typically consisting of eight forwards, who form the scrum and are key in set-piece plays.

Haka: A traditional Maori war dance performed by the New Zealand national rugby team, the All Blacks, before matches, symbolizing strength, unity, and the warrior spirit.

Philanthropy: The practice of actively contributing to the well-being of others, often through charitable initiatives and donations.

Scrum: A method of restarting play in rugby, involving the tight binding of players from both teams in an attempt to gain possession of the ball.

Six Nations Championship: An annual rugby tournament featuring six European teams—

England, France, Ireland, Italy, Scotland, and Wales—competing for the championship title.

Try: The primary method of scoring in rugby, awarded when a player grounds the ball in the opponent's in-goal area.

Twickenham: A famous rugby stadium located in London, England, and often referred to as the home of English rugby.

World Rugby: The international governing body for the sport of rugby, responsible for organizing global competitions, setting rules, and promoting the development of rugby worldwide.

Owen Farrell

Printed in Great Britain
by Amazon